301–307 SOCIOLOGY
EXPANDED VERSION BASED
ON EDITION 19

DDC

DEWEY Decimal Classification®

301–307 Sociology Expanded Version Based on Edition 19

Prepared by

JOHN P. COMAROMI, Editor
DEWEY Decimal Classification
and
MARGARET J. WARREN, Assistant Editor
DEWEY Decimal Classification

FOREST PRESS
A Division of
Lake Placid Education Foundation

85 WATERVLIET AVENUE
ALBANY, NEW YORK 12206 U.S.A.
1982

Library of Congress Cataloging in Publication Data

Dewey, Melvil, 1851–1931.
    Dewey decimal classification. 301–307 Sociology.
    Includes index.
    1. Sociology—Classification. 2. Classification, Dewey decimal. I. Comaromi, John
Phillip, 1937–   . II. Warren, Margaret J. III. Title.

Z696.D72S653 1981   025.4′6301   81–17531

ISBN 0–910608–33–4   AACR2

This book was composed, printed and bound
in the United States of America
at Kingsport Press, Inc., Kingsport, Tennessee

Contents

Publisher's Foreword

The Forest Press Division, Lake Placid Education Foundation, publisher of the DEWEY Decimal Classification, is pleased to provide without charge this expansion of 301–307 Sociology to all purchasers of the 19th edition of the DDC. The expansion was announced as forthcoming in *DC&*, Volume 4, Number 1, June 1980. Literary warrant and requests from the library community justify the expansion, whose numbers will be officially adopted by the Decimal Classification Division and applied to Library of Congress cataloging records as of January 1, 1982.

The Press is aware that this expansion comes only two and a half years after the release of Edition 19. We hope that its publication and distribution indicate a responsiveness on the part of the Press to the responsible organizations and individuals that suggested the revisions.

The Press wishes to acknowledge the editorial work of John P. Comaromi, Editor of the DEWEY Decimal Classification, Margaret J. Warren, Assistant Editor, and Winton E. Matthews, Jr., Decimal Classification Specialist, as well as the commitment of the members of the Forest Press Committee and of the Decimal Classification Editorial Policy Committee to the project.

September 28, 1981

John A. Humphry
EXECUTIVE DIRECTOR
Forest Press

Introduction to the 301–307 Expansion

In response to public demand and at the recommendation of the Decimal Classification Editorial Policy Committee, Forest Press authorized the editors of the Dewey Decimal Classification to expand 301–307 Sociology. The expansion is slightly more than twice the size of the original 301–307 of Edition 19.

Relocations are limited to the following:

(1) Founders, central and local administrative heads, clergy, and missionaries (all formerly 305.6) are now classed in 305.92.
(2) Ethnology, cultural ethnology (formerly 572) are now classed in 306. Physical ethnology remains at 572.
(3) Unwed parenthood (formerly 306.7) is now classed in 306.856.
(4) Group sex (formerly 306.73) is now classed in 306.778.

Historical and geographical treatment of culture and institutions 306.09 has been reinstated in order to provide for cultural and social anthropology of racial, ethnic, and national groups.

In addition to the expansion of 301–307, the editors have provided an index to topics found in the expansion, a comparative table of Edition 18 and Edition 19 (301–307 Expansion) numbers, a manual of application (excerpted from *Manual on the Use of the Dewey Decimal Classification*, Forest Press, 1982), and equivalence tables A and B.

John P. Comaromi, Editor
DEWEY Decimal Classification
Margaret J. Warren, Assistant Editor
DEWEY Decimal Classification

301–307 Expansion

300   Social sciences

The sciences that deal with social activities and institutions

Class here behavioral sciences, social studies

Use 300.1–300.9 for standard subdivisions

Class a specific behavioral science with the subject, e.g., psychology 150; military, diplomatic, political, economic, social, welfare aspects of a war with history of the war, e.g., Vietnamese War 959.7043

For language, see 400; history, 900

301   Sociology

The science that deals generally and comprehensively with social activities and institutions

Class here comprehensive works on society, on anthropology

Class applied sociology in 361–365, a specific aspect of society not provided for in 302–307 with the subject, e.g., general history 900

For specific topics in sociology, see 302–307; cultural and social anthropology, 306; criminal anthropology, 364.2; physical anthropology, 573

[.21]   Folkways

        Class in 390

[.418]   Manuals of sexual technique

        Class in 613.96

[.427 2]   Guides to harmonious family relationships

        Class in 646.78

[.56]   Educational sociology

        Class in 370.19

.7   **Kinds of societies**

        Class specific topics in sociology with respect to specific kinds of societies in 302–307

.72   Nonliterate

.74   Advanced

▶   **302–307   Specific topics in sociology**

Unless other instructions are given, class complex subjects with aspects in two or more subdivisions of this schedule in the number coming last in the schedule, e.g., social deterioration during civil war 303.64 (*not* 303.45); however, class effect of one factor on another with the factor affected, e.g., effect of climate on social change 303.4 (*not* 304.25)

Class comprehensive works in 301

302   Social interaction

Class here social psychology

Class psychology of social influences on individuals in 155.92, of interpersonal relations in 158.2; social psychology of a specific situation with the situation, e.g., psychological effects of overpopulation 304.65

SUMMARY

302.1	**General principles**
.2	**Communication**
.3	**Social interaction in groups**
.4	**Social interaction between groups**
.5	**Relation of individual to society**

[.019]   Psychological principles

         Do not use; class in 302

.072   Research

         Class here sociometry

.1   **General principles**

.12   Social perception

         Including social memory

.13   Social choice

         Including attraction, influence

.14   Social participation

         Including cooperation, competition

.15   Social role (Role theory)

         Including role conflict

.2   **Communication**

         Class here literacy, illiteracy

         Class interdisciplinary works in 001.51

.22   Kinds

         Class media in 302.23

         For language, see 400

.222   Nonverbal communication

.224	Verbal communication
.224 2	Oral
.224 4	Written
.23	Means
.232	Print media
.232 2	Newspapers
.232 4	Periodicals and journals
.234	Mass media

Class here the effect of mass media on society

Class the effect of mass media on a particular group in 305, e.g., on children 305.23; on a particular subject with the subject, e.g., on social change 303.4833

For print media, see 302.232

.234 3	Motion pictures
.234 4	Radio
.234 5	Television
.235	Telephone and telegraph
.24	Content

Examples: information, persuasion, directives

Including rumor

.25	Failures and disorders of communication
.3	**Social interaction in groups**

Class here group decisionmaking processes, negotiation

.33	In abstract and temporary groups

Examples: audiences, crowds, mobs, communities of interest, bus passengers

.34	In small (primary) groups

Groups small enough for all members to engage in face-to-face relationships at one time

Examples: play groups, committees

Class the family in 306.8

.346	Conversation
.35	In hierarchically organized (complex) groups

Example: bureaucracies

.4	**Social interaction between groups**

Including in- and outgroups

.5   **Relation of individual to society**

.52   Reference groups

.54   Individualism

      Class here ambition, aggression

.542   Deviation

.544   Alienation

.545   Isolation

303   Social processes

For social interaction, see 302; relation of natural and quasi-natural factors to social processes, 304

.3   **Coordination and control**

Class here power

For political institutions, see 306.2

.32   Socialization

Indoctrination into and the reinforcement of social behavior

Including social learning

For education, see 370

.323   By the family

.323 1   By the father

.323 2   By the mother

.324   By the school

.325   By religious organizations

.327   By other instrumentalities

Peer groups, play groups, recreational agencies

.33   Social control

For socialization, see 303.32; social control through specific means, 303.34–303.38

▶   303.34–303.38   Social control through specific means

Class comprehensive works in 303.33, socialization through specific means of social control in 303.32

.34   Leadership

Including persuasion, influence, cooperation

.35   Utilitarian control

Use of rewards and incentives

.36   Coercion

> Examples: authority, obedience, restraint, punishment, threat
>
> *For treatment and punishment of offenders, see 364.6*

.37   Normative methods

> *For public opinion, see 303.38*

.372   Customs and belief systems

> Including values

.375   Propaganda

.376   Censorship

> Class censorship programs in 363.31

.38   Public opinion

> Class here attitudes, attitude formation and change
>
> Class propaganda in 303.375; public opinion on a specific subject with the subject, e.g., public opinion on political process 324

.380 72   Research

> Class here measurement of public opinion

.385   Prejudice

> Class prejudices of specific social groupings in 303.387–303.388; prejudices against a specific group in 305

.387   Opinions of specific racial, ethnic, national groups

> Add "Racial, Ethnic, National Groups" notation 1–9 from Table 5 to base number 303.387, e.g., opinions of Chileans 303.3876883; then, unless it is redundant, add 0* and to the result add "Areas" notation 1–9 from Table 2, e.g., the opinions of Chileans in Canada 303.3876883071

.388   Opinions of specific occupational and nonoccupational groupings

> Former heading: Opinions of specific social classes
>
> Add "Persons" notation 04–99 from Table 7 to base number 303.388, e.g., opinions of youth 303.388055; then add 0* and to the result add "Areas" notation 1–9 from Table 2, e.g., the opinions of youth in South Africa 303.388055068

.4   **Social change**

> Class changes in a specific aspect of society with the subject in sociology, e.g., changes in religious institutions 306.6

.42   Gradual change

.43   Discontinuous and disruptive change

---

* Use 00 for standard subdivisions; see instructions at beginning of Table 1

.44   Growth and development

Including progress, specialization

.45   Deterioration and decay

.48   Causes of change

.482   Contact between cultures

Class here acculturation, assimilation; social effects of international assistance, of commerce

.482 09   Historical treatment

Class geographical treatment in 303.4821–303.4829 (*not* 303.482091–303.482099)

.482 1–.482 9   Contact between specific areas

Add "Areas" notation 1–9 from Table 2 to base number 303.482, e.g., cultural exchanges with China 303.48251; then add 0* and again add "Areas" notation 1–9 from Table 2, e.g., cultural exchange between China and Japan 303.48251052

Give priority in notation to the nation emphasized. If the emphasis is equal, give priority to the one coming first in the sequence of area notations

If preferred, give priority in notation to the area requiring local emphasis, e.g., libraries in United States class cultural exchange between the United States and France in 303.48273044

.483   Development of science and technology

.483 2   Transportation

.483 3   Communication

.483 4   Computers

.484   Purposefully induced change

Including social innovation, reform, dissent

Class social welfare services in 361–362

.485   Natural and social disasters

Examples: pandemics, wars

.49   Social forecasts

Class here futurology

Class forecasting in and forecasts of a specific subject with the subject, e.g., the future of the U.S. Democratic Party 324.2736

.490 9   Historical treatment

Class geographical treatment in 303.491–303.499 (*not* 303.49091–303.49099)

---

* Use 00 for standard subdivisions; see instructions at beginning of Table 1

.491–.499	Forecasts for specific areas

Add "Areas" notation 1–9 from Table 2 to base number 303.49, e.g., the Communist bloc in the year 2000 303.491717

.6 **Conflict**

Class conflict in a specific area of social relations with the subject in sociology, e.g., racial conflict 305.8

.61 Civil disobedience

Including passive resistance, nonviolent action

.62 Civil disorder and violence

For civil war and revolution, see 303.64

.623 Riots

.625 Terrorism

Class here activities of urban guerrillas

Class prevention of terrorism in 363.32

.64 Civil war and revolution

Class terrorism in 303.625

.66 War

Including pacifism, sociology of war

Class war as a cause of social change in 303.485, prevention of war in 327.172, legal aspects of war in 341.6, causes of war in 355.027, art and science of warfare in 355–359; military, diplomatic, political, economic, social welfare aspects of a specific war with history of the war, e.g., World War 2 940.53

For civil war, see 303.64

304 **Relation of natural and quasi-natural factors to social processes**

.2 **Human ecology**

Relation of human social activities and institutions to the physical environment

Class here human geography, anthropogeography

.23 Geological factors

.25 Weather and climate

.27 Biological factors

Other than human

.28 Human activity

.282 Pollution

Class comprehensive and interdisciplinary works on pollution in 363.73; a specific aspect of pollution with the aspect, e.g., biological treatment of wastes 628.351

.5　**Genetic factors**

Class here sociobiology (the study of the genetic bases of human social behavior)

Class a specific aspect of sociobiology with the subject in sociology, e.g., the sociobiology of conflict 303.6

.6　**Population**

Class here demography

Class social stratification in 305, population of communities in 307.2

For movement of people, see 304.8

.602 12　Tables, formulas, specifications

Do not use for statistics; class in 312

.61　**Characteristics of populations**

Example: density

.62　**Growth and decline**

Including factors affecting changes in size, e.g., war, plague, economic factors

Class comprehensive works on births and deaths in 304.63

For births, see 304.63; deaths, 304.64

.63　**Births**

Class here comprehensive works on births and deaths

Class the growth and decline of population in 304.62, birth control in 304.66

For deaths, see 304.64

.632　**Fertility**

.634　**Family size**

.64　**Deaths (Mortality)**

.65　**Overpopulation**

Class population control in 304.66, social programs to reduce overpopulation in 363.91

.66　**Population control**

Class here birth control, abortion, infanticide, genocide, sterilization

Class population control programs in 363.9

.662　**Population quality**

.664　**Population quantity**

Including optimum size, zero population growth (ZPG)

.666	Family planning

.8   **Movement of people**

For movement to, from, within communities, see 307.2

.809   Movement from and within specific areas

> Class movement from specific areas to specific areas in 304.83–304.89

.81   Causes

.82   Scale of movement

> Movement of populations to, from, within any area larger than a metropolitan area

> Class movement from and within specific areas in 304.809, to specific areas in 304.83–304.89; political aspects of international movement in 325

.83–.89   Movement to specific areas

> Movement to areas larger than a community, e.g., movement from Maine to California

> Add "Areas" notation 3–9 from Table 2 to base number 304.8, e.g., migration to Australia 304.894; then add 0* and to the result add "Areas" notation 1–9 from Table 2 for place of origin, e.g., migration from United States to Australia 304.894073

305   Social stratification (Social structure)

Social status of, role of, problems of, discrimination against, conflict involving social aggregates, either part of the social structure, e.g., women, middle class; or groupings with definable characteristics that set them slightly apart from the broader society, e.g., handicapped

Class here minorities, subcultures of specific aggregates, equality, inequality

Observe the following table of precedence, e.g., middle class black Roman Catholic male youths 305.235 (*not* 305.31, 305.55, 305.62, or 305.896)

Persons by physical and mental characteristics	305.908
Age levels	305.2
Groups by sex	305.3–305.4
Social classes	305.5
Adherents of religious groups	305.6
Language groups	305.7
Racial, ethnic, national groups	305.8
Various occupational and nonoccupational groupings	305.9 (*except* 305.908)

Class specific problems of, welfare services to social aggregates in 362, a specific aspect of discrimination with the subject, e.g., discrimination in housing 363.51; opinions of specific aggregates in 303.38; the historical experience of a particular group in 930–990

---

* Use 00 for standard subdivisions; see instruction at beginning of Table 1

SUMMARY

305.2	Age levels
.3	Men and women
.4	Women
.5	Social classes
.6	Adherents of religious groups
.7	Language groups
.8	Racial, ethnic, national groups
.9	Various occupational and nonoccupational groupings

▶ **305.2–305.8   Specific elements of social structure**

Class comprehensive works in 305

.2 **Age levels**

Class social services to specific age groups in 362

.23 **Young people**

Through age 20

Class here children

.232 **Infants**

From birth to age two

.233 **Preschool children**

Aged three to five

.234 **School children**

Aged six to eleven

.235 **Adolescents (Young adults)**

Aged twelve to twenty

.24 **Adults**

Class adults of specific sexes in 305.3–305.4

For late adulthood, see 305.26

.242 **Early adulthood**

.244 **Middle adulthood**

.26 **Late adulthood**

Former heading: Adults aged 65 and over

Class the sociology of retirement in 306.38, guides to retirement in 646.79

.3   **Men and women**

Former heading: Men

Including transsexuality

Class here comprehensive and interdisciplinary works on sex role, gender identity

Class sex psychology and psychology of the sexes in 155.3, men and women in late adulthood in 305.26; specific aspects of sex role and gender identity with the subject, e.g., psychology of gender identity 155.33

For women, see 305.4

.31   **Men**

Works emphasizing the male sex

Class here comprehensive and interdisciplinary works on men

Class specific aspects of the sociology of men not provided for here with the subject outside sociology, e.g., legal status of men 346.013

For specific aspects of the sociology of men, see 305.32–305.38

▶   **305.32–305.38   Specific aspects of the sociology of men**

Class comprehensive works in 305.31

.32   **Social role and status of men**

Including consciousness-raising groups for men

Class here men's movements, e.g., men's liberation movement

.33   **Men's occupations**

Add "Persons" notation 09–99 from Table 7 to base number 305.33, e.g., male physicians 305.33616

Class economic aspects of men's occupations in 331

.38   **Specific kinds of men**

.386–.388 **Belonging to various specific religious, language, racial, ethnic, national groups**

Add to base number 305.38 the numbers following 305 in 305.6–305.8, e.g., English-speaking men of South Africa 305.38721068

.389   **Exhibiting various nonoccupational characteristics**

Add to base number 305.389 the numbers following 305.9 in 305.904–305.906, e.g., widowers 305.3890654

.4   **Women**

Class here comprehensive and interdisciplinary works on women

Add to base number 305.4 the numbers following 305.3 in 305.32–305.38, e.g., widows 305.4890654

Class woman suffrage in 324.623, women's education in 376, economic aspects of women's occupations in 331

.5   **Social classes**

         Class here class struggle

         Use of this number for equality and inequality discontinued; class in 305

         Class class struggle in Marxism in 335

.51   General principles

.512   Principles of stratification

.512 2   Caste systems

.513   Social mobility

.52   Upper classes

         Class here aristocracy, elites

.522   By birth

         Class here prominent families

.522 2   Royalty

.522 3   Nobility

.523   By economic status

.523 2   Large landowners and landed gentry

.523 4   Wealthy

         For large landowners, see 305.5232

.524   By political status

         Examples: cabinet ministers, commissars, judges, legislative representatives

.55   Middle classes (Bourgeoisie)

.552   Intelligentsia

.553   Professional classes

         Examples: lawyers, nurses, soldiers, teachers

.554   Managerial and entrepreneurial classes

         Examples: top management, businessmen

         Class farmers in 305.555

.555   Farmers

         Worker-managers who are also landowners

         Including peasant proprietors

         Class agricultural labor in 305.563

.556   White-collar classes

         Examples: clerks, shop assistants, bookkeepers

.56   Lower classes

.562   Laboring classes (Proletariat)

> Employed workers of relatively low pay and social status
>
> Including blue-collar workers
>
> Class agricultural workers in 305.563, slaves in 305.567

.563   Agricultural lower classes

> Examples: agricultural workers, peasants, serfs, sharecroppers
>
> *For peasant proprietors, see 305.555*

.567   Slaves

.568   Alienated and excluded classes

> Examples: hippies, hobos, tramps

.569   The impoverished

.6   Adherents of religious groups

> Add to base number 305.6 the numbers following 2 in "Persons" notation 21–29 from Table 7, e.g., Christian Scientists 305.685; then add 0* and to the result add "Areas" notation 1–9 from Table 2, e.g., Christian Scientists in France 305.685044; however, class founders, central and local administrative heads, clergy, missionaries [*all formerly* 305.6] in 305.92

.7   Language groups

> Add "Languages" notation 1–9 from Table 6 to base number 305.7, e.g., English-speaking people 305.721; then add 0* and to the result add "Areas" notation 1–9 from Table 2, e.g., English-speaking people in South Africa 305.721068

.8   Racial, ethnic, national groups

> Add "Racial, Ethnic, National Groups" notation 01–99 from Table 5 to base number 305.8, e.g., Chinese 305.8951; then, unless it is redundant, add 0* and to the result add "Areas" notation 1–9 from Table 2, e.g., Chinese in the United States 305.8951073

.9   Various occupational and nonoccupational groupings

> Use 305.9001–305.9009 for standard subdivisions
>
> Unless otherwise instructed, class complex subjects with aspects in two or more subdivisions of 305.9 in the number coming last, e.g., socially disadvantaged clergymen 305.92 (*not* 305.90694)

.904   Persons by kinship characteristics

> Add "Persons" notation 043–046 from Table 7 to base number 305.9, e.g., grandchildren 305.90442

---

* Use 00 for standard subdivisions; see instructions at beginning of Table 1

.906   **Persons by cultural level, marital status, sexual orientation, special social status**

.906 3–.906 6   Persons by cultural level, marital status, sexual orientation

> Add "Persons" notation 063–066 from Table 7 to base number 305.9, e.g., widowed persons 305.90654

.906 9   Persons by special social status

> Class criminal offenders in 364.3, convicts in 365

.906 94   Socially disadvantaged persons

> Including war victims, unemployed

> Class persons socially disadvantaged by reason of inclusion in nondominant racial, ethnic, national, socioeconomic, religious groups in 305.5–305.8

.906 947   Unmarried parents

.906 96   Retired persons

.906 97   War veterans

.908   **Persons by physical and mental characteristics**

> Add "Persons" notation 08 from Table 7 to base number 305.9, e.g., gifted persons 305.90829

▶   **305.909–305.99   Persons of various occupational characteristics**

Class comprehensive works in 305.9, men's occupations in 305.33, women's occupations in 305.43

.909   **Generalists and novices**

> Add "Persons" notation 09 from Table 7 to base number 305.9, e.g., bibliographers 305.9091

.91   **Persons occupied with philosophy and related disciplines**

> Add "Persons" notation 1 from Table 7 to base number 305.9, e.g., fortune tellers 305.913

.92   **Persons occupied with religion**

> Founders, central and local administrative heads, clergy, missionaries [*all formerly* 305.6]

> Add "Persons" notation 2 from Table 7 to base number 305.9, e.g., Methodist clergymen 305.927

> Class lay persons adherent to a religion in 305.6

.93–.99   **Persons by other occupational characteristics**

> Add "Persons" notation 3–9 from Table 7 to base number 305.9, e.g., postal workers 305.9383

306   Culture and institutions

The cultural and institutional framework of roles, functions, and patterns within which the groups and members of a society act

Culture: the sum total of a society's beliefs, folkways, mores, science, technology, values, arts

Institutions: general patterns of norms defining behavior in specific social relationships

Class here ethnology, cultural ethnology [*both formerly* 572], ethnography, cultural and social anthropology

Class cultural exchange in 303.482, physical anthropology in 573, the history and social conditions of a specific ethnic group in 930–990

For customs and folklore, see 390

.09   Historical and geographical treatment of culture and institutions

Class the civilization and social conditions of a specific place or group in 909, 930–990

SUMMARY

306.1   Subcultures
.2   Political institutions
.3   Economic institutions
.4   Cultural institutions
.6   Religious institutions
.7   Institutions pertaining to relations of the sexes
.8   Marriage and family
.9   Institutions pertaining to death

.1   Subcultures

Groups sharing the total culture, but also having patterns of behavior peculiar to themselves

Including counterculture, popular culture

Class subcultures of specific aggregates in 305

.2   Political institutions

Institutions concerned with maintaining internal and external peace

Class political science in 320, law in 340, public administration in 350–354

▶   306.23–306.25   Governmental institutions

Class comprehensive works in 306.2

.23   Legislative institutions

.24   Executive institutions

Class military institutions in 306.27, police in 306.28

.25   Judicial institutions

15

.26	Political parties
.27	Military institutions

Class here military sociology

Class military art and science in 355–359

.28	Police

Class police services in 363.2

.3   **Economic institutions**

Social arrangements for production, distribution, consumption

Class social classes in 305.5, specific occupational groupings in 305.9, economics in 330

.32	Property systems

Including kinds of land tenure

.34	Systems of production

Including industrial conflict

.342	Capitalism (Free enterprise)

Class economic aspects in 330.122

.344	Cooperation

Class economic aspects in 334

.345	Socialism

Class political aspects in 320.531, economic aspects in 335

.347	Syndicalism

Class economic aspects in 335.82

.36	Systems of labor

Class here sociology of work, industrial sociology

Class occupational groups in 305.909–305.99, economic aspects of work in 331

.362	Slavery
.363	Indenture
.365	Serfdom
.366	Free systems
.38	Retirement

Class guides to retirement in 646.79

.4   **Cultural institutions**

Including bilingualism

Class educational institutions, sociology of education in 370.19

For religious institutions, see 306.6

.42   Sociology of knowledge

> Including invisible colleges
>
> Class specific instances of the sociology of knowledge in 306.45–306.48

.45   Science

.46   Technology

.47   Art

> Class the sociology of arts and crafts as recreation in 306.489

.48   Recreation

> Class here leisure

.482   Gambling

.483   Sports

> Class gambling on athletic events in 306.482

.484   Music, dance, theater

.485   Television, radio, motion pictures

.487   Hobbies and games

> Class sports in 306.483, gambling on games in 306.482

.488   Reading

.489   Arts and crafts

.6   Religious institutions

> Including sociology of religion
>
> Class social theology in 291.17, Christian social theology in 261, social theology of other religions in 292–299

.7   Institutions pertaining to relations of the sexes

> Class here sexual love, sexual relations
>
> Class unwed parenthood [*formerly* 306.7] in 306.855

.73   Institutional framework

> Class here dating behavior
>
> Class group sex [*formerly* 306.73] in 306.778
>
> *For marriage, see 306.8*

.732   Celibacy

.734   Courtship

.735   Nonmarital relations

> Including ménage à trois
>
> Class extramarital relations in 306.736
>
> *For courtship, see 306.734*

17

.736	Extramarital relations
.737	Illegitimacy
.738	Homosexual marriage
.74	Sexual services (Prostitution)
.742	By females

> Class sexual services by children in 306.745

.743	By males

> Class sexual services by children in 306.745

.745	By children
.76	Sexual orientation

> Class practices connected with specific orientations in 306.77

.762	Neutral
.764	Heterosexual
.765	Bisexual
.766	Homosexual

> Class here gay liberation movement

.766 2	Male
.766 3	Female (Lesbian)
.77	Sexual practices

> Class here copulation, fetishism, transvestism
> Class sexual techniques in 613.96

.772	Masturbation
.773	Sodomy

> *For oral sex, see 306.774*

.774	Oral sex
.775	Sadism

> Class here sado-masochism
> *For masochism, see 306.776*

.776	Masochism
.777	Incest
.778	Group sex [*formerly* 306.73]
.779	Bestiality

.8   **Marriage and family**

Class premarital and marriage counseling in 362.8286; a specific aspect of marriage with the aspect, e.g., wife beating as a crime 364.1555; a specific aspect of the family with the aspect, e.g., how to achieve harmonious family relations 646.78

SUMMARY

306.81	Marriage
.82	Patterns of mate selection
.83	Types of kinship systems
.84	Types of marriage
.85	The family
.87	Intrafamily relationships
.88	Alteration of family patterns
.89	Separation and divorce

.81   **Marriage**

Class homosexual marriage in 306.738, dissolution of marriage in 306.88–306.89

▶   **306.82–306.84   Specific aspects of marriage**

Class comprehensive works in 306.81

.82   **Patterns of mate selection**

Class courtship in 306.734, practical guides to choice of mate and dating behavior in 646.77

.83   **Types of kinship systems**

Patrilineal, matrilineal

.84   **Types of marriage**

Class here second and later marriages

.842   **By number of spouses**

.842 2   Monogamous

.842 3   Polygamous

.843   **Interreligious**

Marriages in which the spouses belong to different religions or different branches of the same religion

.845   **Intercultural**

Class here marriages between citizens of different countries

.846   **Interracial**

.85   **The family**

Including the nonconsanguinal family

Class intrafamily relationships in 306.87, family dissolution in 306.88

.852   **The rural family**

.853	The suburban family
.854	The urban family
.855	The nuclear family

Class the single-parent family in 306.856

.856	The single-parent family

Class here unwed parenthood [*formerly* 306.7]

.857	The extended family
.858	The patriarchal family
.859	The matriarchal family
.87	Intrafamily relationships

Class comprehensive works on family problems and services to families in 362.82, practical guides to harmonious family relationships in 646.78

For alteration of family patterns, see 306.88

.872	Husband-wife

Class manuals of sexual technique in 613.96

.874	Parent-child

Class here the generation gap, stepparent-stepchild relationships

Class child rearing in 649

.874 2	Father-child
.874 3	Mother-child
.875	Sibling

Class here stepbrother and stepsister relationships

.875 2	Brother-brother
.875 3	Brother-sister
.875 4	Sister-sister
.88	Alteration of family patterns

Including desertion, death

For separation and divorce, see 306.89

.89	Separation and divorce

Including binuclear family, shared custody

.9	**Institutions pertaining to death**

Class here interdisciplinary works on death

Class specific aspects of death with the subject, e.g., the psychology of death 155.937

307   Communities

Interacting populations of various kinds of individuals in a common, relatively restricted area

.1   General principles of communities

.12   Planning

Class the physical aspect of city planning in 711

.14   Development

.2   Population

Size, composition; movement to, from, within communities

Including decentralization, resettlement

.3   Structure

Class movement within communities in 307.2

.32   Physical setting

.33   Patterns of use

.332   Industrial

.333   Commercial

.334   Recreational

.336   Residential

Including housing; housing succession

.336 2   Neighborhoods

Class ghettoes in 307.3366

.336 4   Slums

.336 6   Ghettoes

.34   Redevelopment

Class community planning in 307.12

.342   City core

.344   Slum clearance

.346   Parks and recreational facilities

.7   Specific kinds of communities

Class specific aspects of specific kinds of communities in 307.1–307.3

.72   Rural

Including agricultural sociology, rural sociology; plantations

.74   Suburban

.76	Urban

Class here urban sociology

▶ 307.762–307.764   Urban communities by size

Class comprehensive works in 307.76

.762	Small communities
.763	Medium-sized communities
.764	Large communities

Class here metropolitan communities; comprehensive works on cities

For medium-sized communities, see 307.763

▶ 307.766–307.768   Urban communities by kind

Class comprehensive works in 307.76

.766	Mining and industrial towns

Class company towns in 307.767

.767	Company towns
.768	New towns
.77	Self-contained communities
.772	Tribal
.774	Communes

Class kibbutzes in 307.776

.776	Kibbutzes

[308]   [Unassigned]

Most recently used in Edition 16

[309]   [Unassigned]

Most recently used in Edition 18

Index to Topics Found in the 301–307 Expansion

Community	
development	307.14
planning	307.12
redevelopment	307.34
structure	307.3
Company towns	307.767
Competition	302.14
Complex groups	302.35
Computers	
role in soc. change	303.483 4
Conflict	303.6
Consciousness-raising groups	
men's	305.32
women's	305.42
Conurbations	307.764
Conversation	302.346
Cooperation	
economic system	306.344
social	
control	303.4
interaction	302.14
Copulation	306.77
Counterculture	306.1
Courtship	306.734
Crafts	306.489
Cross-cultural studies	306
Crowds	302.33
Cultural	
anthropology	306
ethnology	306
institutions	306.4
processes	306
Culture	306
Customs	
soc. control	303.372
Dance	306.484
Dating	306.73
courtship	306.734
Death	306.9
family dissolution	306.88
Deaths	
demography	304.64
Decay	
soc. change	303.45
Decentralization	
communities	307.2
Degeneration	303.45
Demography	304.6
Desertion	
family dissolution	306.88
Deterioration	
soc. change	303.45
Development	
soc. change	303.44
Deviation	302.542

Disasters	
soc. change	303.485
Discrimination	305
Dissent	
soc. change	303.484
Divorce	306.89
Dying	306.9
Ecology	304.2
Economic institutions	306.3
Economics	
sociology of	306.3
Elites	305.52
Emigration	304.809
Entrepreneurial classes	305.554
Environment, man's	
influence on	304.28
Equality	305
Ethnic groups	305.8
opinions of	303.387
Ethnography	306
Ethnology	306
Excluded classes	305.568
Executive institutions	306.24
Extended	
family	306.857
Extramarital sex relations	306.736
Families	306.85
dissolution	306.88
socialization by	303.323
Family	
dissolution	306.88
planning	304.666
relationships	306.87
size	
demography	304.634
socialization by	303.323
violence	306.87
Farm labor	305.563
Farmers	305.555
Father-child relationships	306.874 2
Fathers	
socialization by	303.323 1
Female	
homosexuals	306.766 3
prostitution	306.742
Fertility	
demography	304.632
Fetishism	306.77
Films *see* Motion pictures	
Forecasting	303.490 28
Forecasts	
social	303.49

Leadership	303.34	New towns	307.768
Legislative institutions	306.23	Newspapers	302.232 2
Leisure	306.48	Nobility	305.522 3
Lesbianism	306.766 3	Nonconsanguinal family	306.85
Literacy		Nondominant aggregates	305
sociology	302.2	Nonliterate societies	301.72
Lower classes	305.56	Nonmarital sex relations	306.735
		Nonverbal communication	302.222
		Nonviolence	303.61
		Normative methods	
Male		soc. control	303.372
homosexuals	306.766 2	Norms	
prostitution	306.743	soc. control	303.372
Managerial classes	305.554	Nuclear family	306.855
Marriage	306.81		
brokerage	306.81		
Masochism	306.776		
Mass media	302.234		
Masturbation	306.772	Obedience	
Mate selection	306.82	soc. control	303.36
Matriarchal family	306.859	Occupational	
Matrilineal kinship	306.83	groups	305.9
Men	305.31	mobility	305.513
Ménage à trois	306.735	Occupations	
Men's		men's	305.33
liberation movement	305.32	women's	305.43
occupations	305.33	Official classes	305.524
Metropolitan communities	307.764	Old age	305.26
Middle classes	305.55	Older adults	305.26
Migration	304.8	Opinion measurement	303.380 72
in communities	307.2	Oral	
Military		communication	302.224 2
institutions	306.27	sex	306.774
sociology	306.27	Organization	302.35
Mining towns	307.766	Orphans	305.23
Minority groups	305	Outgroups	302.4
Minors	305.23	Overpopulation	304.65
Missionaries	305.92		
Mixed marriages	306.843–.846		
Mobs	302.33		
Monogamy	306.842 2	Pacifism	303.66
Mores	306	Pandemics	
Mortality	304.64	effects on population	304.62
Mother-child relationships	306.874 3	soc. change	303.485
Mothers		Parent-child relationships	306.874
socialization by	303.323 2	Parenthood	306.874
Motion pictures	302.234 3	Parks	
recreation	306.485	community development	307.346
role in soc. change	303.483 3	Passive resistance	303.61
Music	306.484	Patriarchal family	306.858
		Patrilineal kinship	306.83
		Peasant proprietors	305.555
		Peasants	305.563
National groups	305.8	Peer groups	
opinions of	303.387	soc. control	303.327
Negotiation	302.3	soc. interaction	302.3
Neighborhoods		Periodicals	302.232 4
communities	307.336 2	Personality and culture	302.5

Sex	
discrimination	305.3–.4
role	305.3
Sexes	
relations of	306.7
Sexism	305.3–.4
Sexual	
love	306.7
orientation	306.76
practices	306.77
relations	306.7
Sexuality	306.7
Sharecroppers	305.563
Shared custody family	306.89
Sibling relationships	306.875
Single-parent family	306.856
Sister-brother relationships	306.875 3
Sisters	
family relationships	306.875 4
Slave labor	306.362
Slavery	306.362
Slaves	305.567
Slum clearance	307.344
Slums	307.336 4
Small groups	302.34
Social	
accommodation	303.6
anthropology	306
change	303.4
choice	302.13
classes	305.5
control	303.33
forecasting	303.49
innovation	303.484
interaction	302
learning	303.32
memory	302.12
mobility	305.513
movements	303.484
perception	302.12
processes	303
psychology	302
role	302.15
sciences	300
status	305
structure	305
Socialism	306.345
Socialization	303.32
Socially disadvantaged	
persons	305.906 94
Society	301
Sociobiology	304.5
Sociology	301
Sociometry	302.072
Sodomy	306.773
Specialization	303.44
Sports	306.483
Stepbrother relationships	306.875

Stepchild-stepparent	
relationships	306.874
Stepparent-stepchild	
relationships	306.874
Stepsister relationships	306.875
Sterilization	304.66
Strikes	306.34
Subcultures	306.1
Suburban	
communities	307.74
families	306.853
Syndicalism	306.347
Technology	306.46
role in soc. change	303.483
Telegraph	302.235
Telephone	302.235
Television	302.234 5
recreation	306.485
role in soc. change	303.483 3
Temporary groups	302.33
Terrorism	303.625
Theater	306.484
Threat	
soc. control	303.36
Towns	307.762
Tradition	306
Tramps	305.568
Transportation	
role in soc. change	303.483 2
Transsexuality	305.3
Transvestism	306.77
Tribal communities	307.772
Unemployed persons	305.906 94
Unions	306.36
Unmarried parents	305.906 947
Untouchables	305.568
Unwed parenthood	306.856
Upper class	305.52
Urban	
communities	307.76
family	306.854
guerrillas	303.625
sociology	307.76
Urbanization	307.76
Values	
cultural aspects	306
soc. control	303.372
Verbal communication	302.224
Veterans	305.906 97

Equivalence Tables

The equivalence tables that follow lead in Table A from Edition 18 numbers to numbers in Edition 19 (301–307 Expansion) for use by persons familiar with the sociology numbers from Edition 18, in Table B from Edition 19 expanded numbers to numbers in Edition 18 for classifiers whose libraries are remaining on Edition 18.

Every number in Edition 18 has an equivalent number or numbers in the Edition 19 expanded version (and vice versa). In most cases, most of the contents of an Edition 18 number will be assigned to the same Edition 19 number in the expanded version. Topics assigned to a different Edition 19 number will be listed separately.

Topics in the subdivisions of an Edition 18 number (and vice versa) will usually travel together to the same Edition 19 number or its subdivisions in the expansion. In cases like this the topics in the subdivisions are not shown. They are shown if they have been transferred to a different number.

The custom of breaking long DDC numbers after every third digit has not been followed in the equivalence tables.

TABLE A

Edition 18	Edition 19 (301–307 Expansion)	Comments
301.04	304	
301.1	302	
301.11	302	
301.112	302.34	
301.113	302.5	
301.113	302.15	Role theory
301.114	302.4	
301.14	302.2	
301.15	303.33	
301.152	303.36	
301.154	303.32	
301.154	303.38	Public opinion
301.1542	303.38072	
301.1543	001–999 with topic	
301.1552	303.36	
301.1553	303.34	
301.1554	302.3	
301.157	303.32	
301.161	302.234	
301.161	302.232	Print media
301.162	302.234	
301.18	302.3	
301.18028	302.072	

TABLE A (Continued)

Edition 18	Edition 19 (301–307 Expansion)	Comments
301.181	302.33	
301.182	302.33	
301.183	302.35	
301.1831	302.3	
301.1832	302.35	
301.185	302.34	
301.2	306	
301.2	301	Anthropology
301.21	306	Beliefs, Mores
301.21	306.4	Language
301.21	306.45	Science
301.21	306.46	Technology
301.21	390	Folkways
301.22	306.1	
301.24	303.4	
301.241	303.482	
301.242	303.484	
301.243	303.483	
301.247–.248	301–307 with topic	
301.31	304.2	
301.32	304.6	
301.32	304.8	Migration
301.32	307.2	Population of communities
301.321	304.632	
301.321	304.63	Births
301.321	304.66	Birth control
301.322	304.64	
301.323	304.61	
301.324	304.8	
301.325–.326	304.809	
301.34	307	
301.35	307.72	
301.35	307.762	Villages
301.351	307.72	
301.352	307.762	
301.36	307.76	
301.36	307.762	Towns
301.361	307	Patterns of growth
301.361	307.2	Migration to cities
301.361	307.3	Community structure
301.362	307.74	
301.363	307.764	
301.364	307.764	
301.4	305	
301.41	305.3	
301.411	305.31	
301.412	305.4	
301.414	306.734	
301.4142	306.73	
301.4143	306.82	

TABLE A (Continued)

Edition 18	Edition 19 (301–307 Expansion)	Comments
301.415	306.736	
301.4152	306.735	
301.4152	306.856	Unwed parenthood
301.4153	306.736	
301.4154	306.74	
301.4157	306.766	
301.4158	306.77	
301.417	306.7	
301.417	306.732	Celibacy
301.418	613.96	
301.42	306.81	Marriage
301.42	306.85	Families
301.4212	306.855	
301.4213	306.857	
301.4222	306.8422	
301.4223	306.8423	
301.426	304.666	
301.427	306.87	
301.4272	646.78	
301.428	306.88	
301.428	306.89	Separation
301.4284	306.89	
301.4286	306.88	
301.429	306.843	Interreligious marriage
301.429	306.845	Intercultural marriage
301.429	306.846	Interracial marriage
301.43	305.2	
301.431	305.23	
301.4314	305.23	
301.4315	305.235	
301.434	305.24	
301.435	305.26	
301.44	305.5	
301.4404	305.513	
301.441	305.5232	Gentry (landed)
301.441	305.5234	Wealthy classes
301.441	305.55	Middle classes
301.441	305.569	Poor classes
301.442	305.5122	
301.442	305.52	Aristocracies
301.442	305.5223	Nobility
301.443	305.5	
301.4442	305.562	
301.4443	305.563	
301.4444	305.55	
301.4445	305.556	
301.4446	305.553	
301.4447	305.554	
301.445	305.552	
301.4492	305.52	
301.4492	305.5222	Royalty

TABLE A (Continued)

Edition 18	Edition 19 (301–307 Expansion)	Comments
301.4493	305.563	Serfs
301.4493	305.567	Slaves
301.4494	305.568	
301.45	305	
301.451	305.8	
301.452	305.6	
301.4528	305.6	
301.4529	305.69	
301.5	306	
301.51	306.3	
301.55	306.36	
301.56	370.19	
301.57	306.48	
301.58	306.6	
301.592	306.2	
301.593	306.27	
301.62	302.542	Deviation
301.62	302.544	Alienation
301.63	303.6	
301.63	305.3–.4	Sexism
301.632	303.61	
301.633	303.62	
301.633	303.625	Terrorism
301.6332	303.623	
301.6333	303.64	
301.6334	303.66	
301.634	306.34	
301.635	305.6	
301.636	305.8	
301.637	305.5	
301.64	303.33	
309.26	307.12	

TABLE B

Edition 19 (301–307 Expansion)	Edition 18	Comments
301	301.2	Anthropology
302	301.11	
302	301.1	Social psychology
302.072	301.18028	
302.15	301.113	
302.2	301.14	
302.232–.234	301.161	
302.3	301.18	
302.3	301.1554	Group decisionmaking
302.33	301.181	Audiences
302.33	301.182	Crowds, Mobs
302.34	301.185	
302.34	301.112	Person-to-person interaction

TABLE B (Continued)

Edition 19 (301–307 Expansion)	Edition 18	Comments
302.35	301.183	
302.4	301.114	
302.5	301.113	
302.542–.544	301.62	
303	301	
303.3	301.15	
303.32	301.157	
303.32	301.154	Indoctrination
303.34	301.1553	
303.36	301.152	
303.36	301.1552	Authority
303.37–.38	301.154	
303.38072	301.1542	
303.4	301.24	
303.482	301.241	
303.483	301.243	
303.484	301.242	Reform, Social innovation
303.6	301.63	
303.61	301.6	
303.61	301.632	Nonviolent action
303.62	301.63	Civil disorder
303.62	301.633	Civil violence
303.623	301.6332	
303.625	301.633	
303.64	301.6333	Revolutions
303.64	301.6334	Civil wars
303.66	301.6334	
304	301.3	
304.2	301.31	
304.5	301.0423	
304.6	301.32	
304.61	301.323	
304.63	301.321	
304.64	301.322	
304.66	301.321	Birth control
304.666	301.426	
304.8	301.32	
304.8	301.324	Immigration
304.809	301.325	Emigration
304.809	301.326	Internal migration
304.83–.89	301.324093–.324099	
305	301.4	
305	301.45	Nondominant aggregrates
305.2	301.43	
305.23	301.431	
305.23	301.4314	Children
305.232–.234	301.4314	
305.235	301.4315	
305.24	301.434	
305.26	301.435	

TABLE B (Continued)

Edition 19 (301–307 Expansion)	Edition 18	Comments
305.3	301.41	
305.31–.38	301.411	
305.4	301.412	
305.5	301.44	
305.5	301.637	Class conflict
305.5122	301.442	
305.513	301.4404	
305.52	301.442	Aristocracies
305.52	301.4492	Elites
305.522	301.442	
305.5222	301.4492	
305.523	301.441	
305.524	301.4492	
305.55	301.441	
305.552	301.445	
305.553	301.4446	
305.554	301.4447	
305.555	301.4443	
305.556	301.4445	
305.56	301.441	
305.562	301.4442	
305.563	301.4443	
305.563	301.4493	Serfs
305.567	301.4493	
305.568	301.4494	
305.6	301.452	
305.6	301.635	Religious conflict
305.7	301.45	
305.8	301.451	
305.8	301.636	Racial conflict
305.9	301.45	
306	301.2	Culture
306	301.21	Beliefs, Mores
306	301.5	Institutions
306.1	301.22	
306.2	301.592	
306.27	301.593	
306.3	301.51	
306.34	301.634	Industrial conflict
306.36	301.55	
306.4	301.5	
306.4	301.21	Language
306.45–.46	301.21	
306.48	301.57	
306.6	301.58	
306.7	301.41	
306.73	301.4142	Dating
306.732	301.417	
306.734	301.414	
306.736	301.415	

TABLE B (Continued)

Edition 19 (301–307 Expansion)	Edition 18	Comments
306.737	301.4152	
306.738	301.415	
306.74	301.4154	
306.76	301.417	
306.766	301.4157	
306.77	301.4158	
306.77	301.417	Copulation
306.8	301.42	
306.82	301.4143	
306.83	301.421	
306.84	301.422	
306.8422	301.4222	
306.8423	301.4223	
306.843–.846	301.429	
306.852–.854	301.421	
306.855	301.4212	
306.856	301.421	
306.856	301.4152	Unwed parenthood
306.857	301.4213	
306.858–.859	301.421	
306.87	301.427	
306.88	301.428	Desertion
306.88	301.4286	Death
306.89	301.421	Binuclear family, Shared custody
306.89	301.428	Separation
306.89	301.4284	Divorce
306.9	301.5	
307	301.34	
307.12	309.26	
307.2–.3	301.35	Rural communities
307.2–.3	301.361	Urban communities
307.72	301.35	
307.74	301.362	
307.76	301.36	
307.762	301.35	Villages
307.762	301.352	Agricultural villages
307.762	301.36	Towns
307.763	301.363	
301.764	301.363	Cities
307.764	301.364	Metropolitan communities

Comparative Table of Numbers in Edition 18 and Edition 19 (301–307 Expansion)

	Edition 18	Edition 19 (301–307 Expansion)
Acculturation	301.241	303.482
Adolescents	301.431 5	305.235
Adultery	301.415 3	306.736
Adults	301.434	305.24
Age levels	301.43	305.2
Aged persons	301.435	305.26
Agricultural classes		
lower	301.444 3	305.563
sociology	301.35	307.72
villages	301.352	307.762
Alienated classes	301.449 4	305.568
Alienation	301.62	302.544
Anthropology	301.2	301
Audiences	301.181	302.33
mass media	301.162	302.234
Authority		
soc. control	301.155 2	303.36
Beliefs	301.21	306
Birth control	301.321	304.66
Births	301.321	304.63
Books	301.161	302.232
Bureaucracies	301.183 2	302.35
Change	301.24	303.4
Children	301.431 4	305.23
Choice of mate	301.414 3	306.82
Cities	301.363	307.764
Class conflict	301.637	305.5
Cliques	301.185	302.34
Coercion		
soc. control	301.152	303.36
Committees	301.185	302.34
Communication	301.14	302.2
Communities	301.34	307
Community		
structure	301.361	307.3
Conflict	301.63	303.6
Conurbations	301.364	307.764
Courtship	301.414	306.734
Crowds	301.182	302.33
Cultural		
anthropology	301.2	306
processes	301.2	306
Culture	301.2	306

	Edition 18	Edition 19 (301–307 Expansion)
Dating	301.414 2	306.73
courtship	301.414	306.734
Deaths		
demography	301.322	304.64
Demography	301.32	304.6
Desertion		
family dissolution	301.428	306.88
Deviation	301.62	302.542
Divorce	301.428 4	306.89
Ecology	301.31	304.2
Economic institutions	301.51	306.3
Elites	301.449 2	305.52
Emigration	301.325	304.809
Entrepreneurial classes	301.444 7	305.554
Ethnic groups	301.451	305.8
Excluded classes	301.449 4	305.568
Extended family	301.421 3	306.857
Extramarital sex relations	301.415 2–.415 4	306.736
Families	301.42	306.85
Family		
dissolution	301.428	306.88
planning	301.426	304.666
relationships	301.427	306.87
Fertility		
demography	301.321	304.632
Gangs	301.185	302.34
Gentry (landed)	301.441	305.523 2
Governing classes	301.449 2	305.52
Group		
decisionmaking	301.155 4	302.3
Groups	301.18	302.3
Hippies	301.449 4	305.568
Hobos	301.449 4	305.568
Homosexuality	301.415 7	306.766
Human		
ecology	301.31	304.2
Husband-wife relationships	301.427	306.872
Immigration	301.324	304.83–.89
Individualism	301.113	302.54
Indoctrination	301.154	303.32–.33
Industrial		
conflict	301.634	306.34
Ingroups	301.114	302.4
Institutions	301.5	306
Intellectuals	301.445	305.552
Intelligentsia	301.445	305.552
Internal migration	301.326	304.809
International assistance		
soc. effects of	301.241	303.482
Intrafamily relations	301.427	306.87
Isolation	301.113	302.545

	Edition 18	Edition 19 (301–307 Expansion)
Laboring classes	301.444 2	305.562
Language		
cultural institution	301.21	306.4
Leadership	301.155 3	303.34
Managerial classes	301.444 7	305.554
Marriage	301.42	306.81
Mass media	301.161	302.234
Men	301.411	305.31
Metropolitan communities	301.364	307.764
Middle classes	301.441	305.55
Migration	301.324–.328	304.8
Military		
institutions	301.593	306.27
Minority groups	301.45	305
Minors	301.431	305.23
Mobs	301.182	302.33
Monogamy	301.422 2	306.842 2
Mores	301.21	306
Mortality	301.322	304.64
Motion pictures	301.161	302.234 3
National groups	301.451	305.8
Newspapers	301.161	302.232 2
Nobility	301.442	305.522 3
Nondominant aggregates	301.45	305
Nonviolence	301.632	303.61
Nuclear family	301.421 2	306.855
Official classes	301.449 2	305.524
Opinion measurement	301.154 2	303.380 72
Outgroups	301.114	302.4
Parent-child relationships	301.427	306.874
Peasants	301.444 3	305.563
Periodicals	301.161	302.232 4
Plantations	301.35	307.72
Play groups		
soc. interaction	301.185	302.34
Political		
institutions	301.592	306.2
Polygamy	301.422 3	306.842 3
Population		
communities	301.32	307.2
decline	301.32	304.62
growth	301.32	304.62
movement	301.324–.328	304.8
Poor classes	301.441	305.569
Premarital relations	301.415 2	306.735
Primary groups	301.185	302.34
Prostitution	301.415 4	306.74
Public opinion	301.154	303.38
Publics	301.181	302.33
Racial		
conflict	301.636	305.8

	Edition 18	Edition 19 (301–307 Expansion)
Racism	301.636	305.8
Radio	301.161	302.234 4
Recreational		
institutions	301.57	306.48
Reform	301.242	303.484
Religious		
conflicts	301.635	305.6
groups	301.452	305.6
institutions	301.58	306.6
Revolutions	301.633 3	303.64
Riots	301.633 2	303.623
Role		
theory	301.113	302.15
Royalty	301.449 2	305.522 2
Rural		
communities	301.35	307.72
sociology	301.35	307.72
Science	301.21	306.45
role in social change	301.243	303.483
Secondary groups	301.183	302.35
Separation	301.428	306.89
Serfs	301.449 3	305.563
Sexism	301.6	305.3–.4
Sharecroppers	301.444 3	305.563
Slaves	301.449 3	305.567
Small groups	301.185	302.34
Social		
anthropology	301.2	306
classes	301.44	305.5
innovation	301.242	303.484
interaction	301.11	302
mobility	301.440 4	305.513
psychology	301.1	302
status	301.4	305
Socialization	301.157	303.32
Sociometry	301.180 28	302.072
Subcultures	301.22	306.1
Suburban		
communities	301.362	307.74
Technology	301.21	306.46
role in soc. change	301.243	303.483
Television	301.161	302.234 5
Terrorism	301.633	303.625
Towns	301.36	307.762
Tramps	301.449 4	305.568
Untouchables	301.449 4	305.568
Unwed parenthood	301.415 2	306.856
Urban		
communities	301.36	307.76
sociology	301.36	307.76
Villages	301.35	307.762

Comparative Table

	Edition 18	Edition 19 (301–307 Expansion)
Violence	301.633	303.62
Voluntary associations	301.183 1	302.3
War		
soc. conflict	301.633 4	303.66
Wealthy classes	301.441	305.523 4
White-collar classes	301.444 5	305.556
Women	301.412	305.4

Manual of Application for the 301–307 Expansion*

300 Social sciences

The social sciences deal with the basic human structures and activities that enable people to live together and to produce the necessities and amenities of existence. They cover virtually every aspect of human activity except the technological and artistic. Even language 400 is sometimes considered to be a social science. Most of the social sciences are found in 300–399, but one of the most important, history, is found in 900 (considered by some to belong to the humanities). They are fluid and ever changing, the boundaries between one discipline and another are overlapping and far from clear. Without a doubt, the social sciences constitute the most difficult area in which to classify.

Sociology 301–307 is the study of the processes, interactions, groups, and institutions that give form and purpose to every society. Part of the subject matter of sociology is found in 390 Customs, etiquette, folklore.

Much of the raw data for the study of human society is found in 310 Statistics.

In order to maintain internal peace and safety from external threat, societies devise political processes and institutions such as the state and the government. These are dealt with in 320 Political science and in 350–354, which deal with the executive branch of government and public administration. The military arm of government is found in 355–359.

The production, distribution, and consumption of the goods and services needed to maintain society are dealt with in 330 Economics. Part of this discipline is also found in 380–382, that part which deals with commerce and trade. Also found in the 380s are two of the major auxiliaries to commerce, communication 383–384 and transportation 385–388.

Law 340 treats the codified social, political, and economic rules that society requires and by which its members agree to live.

No social structure, however good, is perfect, and social problems are inevitable. The nature of these problems, taken together with the services society performs to overcome them, are dealt with in the 360s.

Education 370 is the science and art through which society attempts to socialize the young and to prepare them for a useful role in the life of the society.

---

* Excerpted from *Manual on the Use of the Dewey Decimal Classification* (Forest Press, 1982).

300 vs. 600   Social sciences vs. Technology

Many topics can be discussed from either a technological or a social point of view. Determining which point of view a work takes is sometimes difficult.

If a work discusses how to make, operate, maintain, or repair something, it is usually classed in technology. If, on the other hand, it discusses the social implications of a technological operation, it falls in the social sciences, e.g., the economic importance of lumbering 338.174982, not 634.982.

Class social utilization, social control, and the social effect of technology in 300. The distinction between social science and technology is especially difficult for works emphasizing the interface between technology and its use or control, works that fall somewhere along the continuum from technology at one end to social science at the other. This is particularly true of regulatory control *(see 363.1 Public safety programs and 363.7 Environmental problems and services)* and popular works *(see 385–388 Specific kinds of transportation).*

The following criteria will be useful in determining that material should be classed in 300 rather than in 600:

1. When the emphasis is on social use rather than on operating or further processing, e.g., tea drinking in England 394.12, not 641.33720942 or 641.63720942.

2. When the emphasis is on the overall perspective, e.g., the shift from coal to oil in American industry 333.82130973, not 621.4023.

3. When the emphasis is on social control as opposed to the control exercised during the manufacturing process, e.g., standards of drug quality imposed by a government agency or a trade association 363.1946, not 615.19.

4. When the raw statistics are cited, e.g., crop production, acreage, fertilizer use, farm size 338.1, not 631.

Technical reports

Many technical reports and research reports actually emphasize procedural technicalities and may refer to economic, legal, administrative, or regulatory complexities and should, therefore, be classed in the social sciences. In determining the classification of a report series, and of individual reports in a series, consider the mission of the agency authorizing the reports and the purpose of the writer. If the emphasis is on the exercise of social control over a process, the report is classed in 300, not with the process in technology which is being controlled. For example, water quality monitoring systems are more likely to be at 363.739463 than at 628.161. *(See also notes on control of technology under 363, on safety regulations under 363.1, on water reports under 363.61.)*

It cannot be stressed too strongly that many or most of the social sciences are involved in technological processes but are quite distinct from them. The classifier must go behind the technological vocabulary that often dominates title pages and tables of contents and analyze what is being described. A book on trains is not classed in 625.2 if it describes how railroads serve Argentina, but at 385.0982; and a report on fertilizer and rice is not classed at 633.18891 if it is studying production efficiency in developing countries, but at 338.162.

Comprehensive works

Generally speaking, the 300 number is the comprehensive number for a phenomenon of social significance; it is used as the place of last resort for general works on a subject lacking disciplinary focus, e.g., a work on industrial archaeology not emphasizing how things were made 338.47609 rather than 609. However, works that emphasize descriptions of products or structures, such as clocks, locomotives, windmills, are classed in technology.

Biography and company history

Works on artisans, engineers, and inventors are normally classed in technology. Works on artisans, engineers, and inventors who are of more interest as entrepreneurs are classed in 338.7, e.g., Henry Ford 338.762920924.

Many works on products concentrate on the products of specific companies, e.g., Seth Thomas clocks or Ferrari automobiles. So long as these works emphasize the description and design of the products, class them in technology (or art 700 if the interest is artistic). But as soon as the organization or history of the company receives significant attention, class in 338.7, e.g., Seth Thomas clocks 681.113097461, but the Seth Thomas Clock Company and its clocks 338.7681113097461.

301–307   **Sociology**

Sociology is the description and analysis of social phenomena, i.e., of group behavior. Even if the social phenomena being studied take place in a special context, e.g., in a political or economic institution, the work is classed in 301–307. For instance, a descriptive work on family patterns of members of the executive branch of government is classed at 306.87; on the social role of political institutions in Korea at 306.209519; on the use of power among committee chairmen of a national legislature at 306.23.

The description and analysis of the group behavior that occurs in a specific place is classed with the specific social behavior, if any, plus notation for any nondominant group rather than in the number for the place, e.g., patterns of mate selection among Jews in Los Angeles 306.82089924079494.

Sociology and anthropology

Sociology and anthropology cover much of the same territory and are classed in the same numbers. General works on anthropology are classed in 301. Different branches of anthropology are classed as follows: Physical anthropology is concerned with the biological aspects of being human and is classed in 573. Cultural and social anthropology deal with culture and institutions and are classed in 306. Criminal anthropology is classed in 364.2.

Structure of 301–307

All societies are composed of an environment that affects their development (304), of social processes that must be maintained so the society can continue to exist (303), of social groupings of persons that in one configuration or another carry on the processes that make society possible (305), of culture and institutions that are the framework (roles, functions, patterns) within which the groups carry on the processes (306), and of communities (307).

302 Social interaction contains basic forms of behavior between individuals in groups and between groups; these forms are basic to all other forms of social behavior.

Comprehensive works on all aspects of society are classed in 301.

Citation order

Unless otherwise instructed, e.g., at 305, when more than one topic is involved, class a work with the topic coming later in the schedule, e.g., the role of communication in economic institutions 306.3, not 302.2; the role of mass media in socializing

Cuban immigrants 305.8687291, not 303.32 or 302.234. However, class the effect of one element upon another with the element affected, e.g., the effect of religious opinions on birth control practices among upper class white women 304.66, not 305.4, 305.52, 305.8034, 303.38, or any number in the 200s; the effect of school desegregation patterns on housing patterns in three Eastern U.S. cities 307.336, not 370.19342 (there is a note to 370.19 from 306.4), and not 305.896073; effect of television violence on children 305.23, not 302.2345 or 302.24.

301–306 vs. 361–365 [Sociology] vs. Social problems and services

To be classed in 301–306 works on social phenomena must deal exclusively, or almost exclusively, with the phenomenon in its pure state, i.e., its social background, its role in the social structure, its effects on society, its innate characteristics and inner structure.

Consideration of social pathology apart from remedial measures is often found in 301–306, although social pathology is more likely to be found in the 361–365 span. The family as a social phenomenon is classed in 306.85. The dissolution of the family can be classed in either 306.88 or 362.82 depending on the focus of the work. A work discussing the effect of the changing social role of women in bringing about family dissolution is classed at 306.88. Once this topic begins to be considered as a problem about which something should be done the work is classed in 362.82, e.g., what should be done to prevent family dissolution 362.827. The case for a 361–365 number is even stronger when remedial measures are considered, e.g., counseling services for families in trouble 362.8286.

It is even possible to find remedial measures discussed purely as social phenomena. Birth control, for example, can be discussed in terms of its prevalence in various social strata, in terms of its actual effect on population growth, in terms of public attitudes toward it. Such a discussion is classed at 304.66. However, the use of birth control as a social remedy is classed at 363.96. A work on remedial measures, of course, is even more likely to be found in applied than in pure sociology.

If in doubt, prefer 361–365. This means, of course, that 361–365 will be much more heavily used than 301–306. Many topics classed in 301 in Edition 18 and previous editions will now be classed in 361–365.

It should be noted that the above does not apply to criminology. Here both pure and applied sociology are to be classed in 364 as indicated by the note at 364.2 in Edition 19, "Class here criminal anthropology."

301.019   [Psychological principles of sociology]

Class social psychology in 302.

301.09   **[Historical and geographical treatment of sociology]**

Class here regional sociology.

302 vs. 150   **[Social psychology] vs. Psychology**

See discussion at 150 vs. 302–307.

302.24   Content [of communication]

Including censorship.

Class persuasion from the psychological standpoint at 153.852.

303.4   **Social change**

Class forecasting in 003.2; the effect of one aspect of change on another with the aspect being affected, e.g., social change brought about by change in climate 303.485, but the effect of human activities in changing the climate 304.25.

303.482   Contact between cultures

Class intercultural education in 370.196.

303.484   Purposefully induced change

Reform movements here are considered as social phenomena.

Class the political aspects of reform movements at 322.44, the role of reform movements in relation to a social problem in 361–365.

303.6   **Conflict**

Conflict as a social phenomenon.

Class the history of major conflicts in 900, e.g., the Miami race riot of 1980 975.9381063.

Class political aspects of conflicts in 320.

See 322.4 and 322.42.

304.2   **Human ecology**

The effect of natural factors on the social order in general, e.g., the role of such things as mountains, plains, tropical climate, prevailing winds, prevalence of volcanoes in shaping social activity, order, structure.

Class environmental policy at 363.70525.

304.28   Human activity [in relation to ecology]

Planning to combat pollution is classed with the problem at 363.73525.

304.6   Population (Demography)

Class statistics of population in 312.

304.66   Population control

Class programs and discussions of social policy at 363.96; personal practices and techniques of birth control in 613.94.

305   Social stratification (Social structure)

Social structure treats the division of society by kinds of people according to their age, sex, religion, language, race, or by any other characteristic that forms a definable grouping.

Frequently it will prove difficult to distinguish between a description of the social life of a group and a discussion of the institution of which the group is inextricably a part, e.g., slaves as a social grouping 305.567, slavery as an economic institution 306.362; soldiers as a social grouping 305.9355, military institutions 306.27. When related groups and institutions are discussed equally in a work, class the work in 306. If in doubt, prefer 306.

305.3   Men and women

Class relations between the sexes and within the sexes in 306.7–306.8, the relation of a specific sex to a specific subject with the subject, using s.s. 088041–088042, e.g., women in U.S. history 973.088042.

305.42   [Social role and status of women]

Class here feminism as a social phenomenon. Class programs and policies to promote the welfare of women in 362.83.

305.43   [Occupations of women]

Class here works that treat the sociological aspects of women's relation to labor, e.g., how work has affected the position and role of women in society, how jobs are changing so that women are being affected, how women regard work, and social views of women's occupations.

Class economic aspects of the relation of women to labor in 331.4.

305.569   The impoverished

Class problems of and services to the poor in 362.5.

305.8   **Racial, ethnic, national groups**

Class here racial, ethnic, national groups only to illustrate their social behavior and the history of the behavior. Class works treating the history and civilization of such groups in 900, e.g., a history of the Australian aborigines 994.0049915.

306   **Culture and institutions**

The structural elements here are the functions performed rather than the kind of people involved; it is the framework within which the members of the various groups act.

In the expansion of 301–307, 306.09 Historical and geographical treatment of culture and institutions was reinstated. This number is used for the anthropological and sociological works that deal with the social mechanics and social causation of the cultural and social life in a specific place. However, class the history of a particular group and its civilization in 909 or 930–990 when it is focusing on the social history of the place or the work is considered to be a contribution to the social history of the place. Thus ethnographic works can be classed in either 305–306 or 909, 930–990, depending upon the focus of the author, his field of study, and his intended audience. If in doubt, prefer 900.

The following table explains the distribution of works on social groups:

General anthropology	301
Physical anthropology	573
Criminal anthropology	364
Cultural and social anthropology	306
Cultural ethnology (culture of races in general)	306
Physical ethnology (physical characteristics of races)	572
Ethnography (cultural and social anthropology of specific groups)	
As part of the general society of a place	305
Not as part of the general society of a place	306.089
Historical ethnography	909, 930–990
Civilization of any group	909, 930–990
Social conditions of a group	909, 930–990, 305

306.1   Subcultures

Including the drug culture: a subculture that shares the belief that the use of drugs is legitimate, a norm not approved by the dominant culture. Any emphasis on the problems the drug culture causes the larger society points to the use of 362.293, social problems and services connected with addiction.

306.3   Economic institutions

Class sociology of housing in 307.336.

306.6   Religious institutions

These must be treated from a secular, nonreligious viewpoint.

306.7   Institutions pertaining to relations of the sexes

Class here the sexual behavior and habits of a specific group, using s.s. 088, e.g., sexual behavior of adolescents 306.7088055. Class sexual ethics in 176, problems and controversies concerning various relations in 363.4, sex offenses in 364.153, sexual customs at 392.6, sex hygiene in 613.95, manuals on sexual techniques at 613.96, sex practices viewed as treatable disorders in 616.8583.

306.74   Sexual services (Prostitution)

Class prostitution as an occupation at 331.76130674, as a social problem in 363.44, as a trade at 380.14530674; biographies of prostitutes, madams, and pimps in 306.74092.

306.85   The family

Class the psychology of family influences at 155.924. If in doubt regarding a work dealing with both the psychology of family influences and the patterns of family relationships, prefer 306.85.

307   Sociology of communities

This section is a combination of sociology and the applied social sciences. It includes works on the community as a social phenomenon and works on community planning and development. These terms are used here in their ordinary meaning to imply the planning for and development of the community as a whole. When specific subjects of community interest are addressed, the work is classed elsewhere in 300, e.g., economic development of the community 338.93–338.99, developing hospitals for the community 362.11, planning community housing 363.5525, planning the city water supply 363.61, planning the education system 379.4–379.9.

Class the psychology of community influences in 155.94. If in doubt whether a work should be classed in the psychology of community influences (155.94) or the social psychology of communities (307), prefer 307.

307 vs. 900 **Sociology of communities vs. General geography and history and their auxiliaries**

The description of such aspects of a community as population, size, residential patterns, kinds of neighborhoods is classed in 307, not in 900. For instance, urban renewal in London is classed at 307.3409421. However, when economic, political, and other social science aspects are included, such as are found in works on social conditions, the work is classed in 900, e.g., London in the third quarter of the 20th century 942.1085.

307.72 Rural [communities]

Note that "rural" does not necessarily mean agricultural; it means here country rather than city environment.

Class villages in 307.762.